Timothy Earle

# An Essay on Political Economies in Prehistory

Graduiertenkolleg 1878
Beiträge zur Wirtschaftsarchäologie
Band 2

gefördert durch die DFG

 Deutsche
Forschungsgemeinschaft

Herausgegeben von
Martin Bentz – Michael Heinzelmann

Die Deutsche Nationalbibliothek verzeichnet diese Publikation
in der Deutschen Nationalbibliografie;
detailliertere bibliografische Daten sind im Internet
über ‹http://dnb.dnb.de› abrufbar.

Gestaltung und Satz: Dietmar Hofmann

Druck: druckhaus köthen GmbH & Co. KG

© 2017 Habelt-Verlag, Bonn
Dr. Rudolf Habelt GmbH, Am Buchenhang 1, 53115 Bonn

ISBN 978-3-7749-4115-1

# Contents

# Foreword

October through December 2015, I was a Mercator Fellow at the Universities of Cologne and Bonn. This paper summarizes my advanced seminar presentations there for the DFG Research Training Group (RTG 1878) "Archaeology of Pre-Modern Economies". I presented my theoretical understanding of the political economy as helping explain archaeological variation in power and social inequality. My argument grew out of a series of article and books (especially Artursson et al. 2016; Earle 1997, 2002, 2017b; Earle and Spriggs 2015; Earle et al. 2015), and much of this essay summarizes this earlier work. As an essay summarizing my understanding, I do not provide the full references that can be found in my other publications. I am grateful for the intense and thoughtful discussion that I had in Germany with the faculty and post-graduate students. Among the academic staff, I particularly valued discussions with Martin Bentz and Michael Heinzelmann, organizers of the training group. Tobias Kienlin, Sabine Schrenk, and Andreas Zimmermann were my interlocutors, bringing fresh ideas to my thinking. I appreciated very much my discussions with post-doctoral fellows Tim Kerig concerning labor as the key variable with which to compare prehistoric economies and Giorgos Papantoniou about ritual economies. Tim Kerig was my editor, giving thoughts and good advice on an earlier manuscript. And then there was Ina Borkenstein; she was absolutely essential, supporting my relaxed and productive stay in Germany. I could not be more grateful for her assistance and cheerful personality. After my time in Germany, I was a visiting scholar at Gothenburg University, Sweden. With Johan Ling and Kristian Kristiansen, I wrote a conference paper there on the political economy of Bronze Age Scandinavian chiefdoms (Ling et al. 2016), which has been revised and submitted to Current Anthropology. I incorporate ideas from that manuscript here.

# Introduction

To understand pre-modern economies is vital to understanding the long-term organization, operation and development of human societies. Economies are foundational. They are the totality of material processes involving production, distribution and consumption of things and services. Everything that is social is at the same time partially economic, involving provisioning, cooperation and command, governance, and religious practices. Human populations require subsistence, organizational structure, and meaning in their lives, and all these are materially based. Whether the family meal, the community feast, symbols of cultural identity, political activities, or pan-regional religious ceremonials, all require material support for their realization. Karl Polanyi (1957) called these economic processes 'provisioning', the structured flow of resources to support human activities. He was reacting to a 20th century trend in economic theory to reduce studies of economies to a formal logic of maximization, the theory of microeconomics. Polanyi rather saw economies as fundamentally structured to maintain the substance of a group – its long-term stability within its natural and cultural environments. Spawned by Polanyi, the 'substantivist' school of economic anthropology studies how traditional economies include gift exchange and redistribution that were deeply embedded in social structure (Dalton 1969, 1977; Sahlins 1972).

Substantivism was part of a broader theoretical approach in anthropology called 'structural functionalism', in which social components, in ways analogous to the organs of a body, were thought to function to maintain social structures (Malinowski 1944; Radcliffe-Brown 1952). A weakness of structural functionalism, however, was its conception of traditional societies as operating for the general good (maintenance of the cultural system), without understanding the competing interests of different social segments. For example, Polanyi ignored social divisions into classes with distinct interests and power. What was missing from Polanyi's analysis was the political economy approaches of the 19th century and Marx's analysis in particular. Economic approaches that investigated institutional order should also investigate how economic relationships translate into power. As is understood for modern society, control over the economy renders power over people and creates inequality.

Political power and social inequality were artifacts of human craft. From the writings of Adam Smith (1937 [1776]) and Ricardo (1817), the structure of the political economy was seen as benefiting some more than others in a class system, whereby capitalists received profits, laborers received wages, and landowners received rents. As long as market conditions were 'free', the overall productivity of the system should result in a rapid equilibration in efficiency and productivity that would benefit all. By 'free', Adam Smith meant a market system without the monarch's patronage for his supporters, to whom he offered monopolies, such as for imported wines. Profits in a free market theoretically induce people to enter an advantageous sector of production and trade, which increases competition and lowers profits to the benefit of all. As the scale of economic firms increased, however, with expanding capital technology and means of finance and transportation, markets became fundamentally unfree, as monopolies emerged based on high capital costs for entering particular industries. Marx (1967) realized that private property in capitalist firms created new monopolies, by which robber barons could accumulate vast wealth at the expense of powerless laborers. The result of capitalism with its large-scale firms led dramatically to increased class inequality. Marx intended to provide scientific (not faith-based) analysis that could revolutionize human society by breaking the privileges of private property.

Could such an elegant analysis be applied to the emergence of power and economy in prehistory? In *Formen, die der kapitalistischen Produktion vorhergehen*, Marx (1965) discussed the historical formations that emerged with different economic systems. A political economy approach to prehistory must strip away the specifics of capitalism, such that a generalized political economy approach can provide tools for understanding how power strategies were built on economic control (Earle 1997; Earle and Spriggs 2015). "Just as Darwin discovered the law of development of organic nature, so Marx discovered the law of development of human history" (Engels 1883). A Marxist analysis of the political economy in prehistory requires the identification of conditions responsible for emergent political control and social stratification. Marx believed that change must be understood in terms of historical materialism, the specific economic conditions that allow the domination of one group (class) over another. Historical materialism never entails a simple reduction to economic factors, because economic relations were structured socially and politically. Fundamental to developing political systems were alternative modes of production that organized technology, property and social relations for political control or its resistance (Marx 1965).

Marx (1965), Engels (1972) and the Marxist archaeologist V. Gordon Childe (1942, 1951; Trigger 1980; Patterson 2009) have all developed general schemes of sociopolitical change across the *longue durée* of human history. The problems with their schemes were not their logic, which was based on general principles of political economy, but rather with difficulties derived from poor historical and archaeological evidence. With the scientific revolutions in archaeology and with the impressive accumulation of new prehistoric evidence, the possibility exists to renew a political economy approach to prehistory. This approach should not, however, produce yet another typological scheme of unilinear evolution (Neitzel and Earle 2014). Rather archaeologists can best focus on process by proposing and evaluating models for how human societies change across the *longue durée*. Such models should not be confused with factual accounts or typologies; rather they are theory-based formulations that can guide future research.

The literature on political economy and Marxism is vast and well beyond the scope appropriate here for review. Approaches to political economy in prehistory have already been quite well developed, suggesting alternative ways that social, political, and economic relationships are linked (Earle and Spriggs 2015; McGuire 2008; Spriggs 1984). The common feature of political economy analysis is that different social segments have distinct and often competing interests and that structural positions in the economy create differential power relationships. Although apparent in highly stratified societies, elements exist even in relatively egalitarian communities (Cobb 1994; Saitta 2005). A related approach is collective action theory, in which a political economy can be viewed as a dynamic negotiation between groups to further their specific interests, rather than a top-down relationship of control (Blanton and Fargher 2008; Carballo et al. 2014). In her book *Of Rule and Revenue*, Levi (1988) develops her theory of 'predatory rule', suggesting that while all elites try to maximize power through revenue extraction, their ability to do so depends on the specifics of resource flows. In corporate strategies (Blanton et al. 1996), for example, because surplus derives from their local population, agricultural communities can negotiate favorable conditions.

My focus is on one aspect of the equation – how to operationalize the concentration of power resulting from bottlenecks that allow agents to channel resource flows and thus mobilize resources for their support.

"Bottlenecks are constriction points in commodity chains that offer an aspiring leader the opportunity to limit access, thus creating ownership over resources, technologies, or knowledge. Ownership facilitates the extraction of surpluses as corvée labor, rent, or other payments that fund power strategies" (Earle and Spriggs 2015: 517). Bottlenecks are both the intended consequence of agents to enforce limitations, such as the building of fortification to exclude others, or the unintended consequence of the developing resource flows in the general economy, such as with intensification of production or trade. Any bottleneck is not absolute; for example, to be effective, ownership of land requires a circumscribed population that cannot vote with its feet, moving to open lands elsewhere or control of a trade route without reasonable alternatives.

To construct political economy models to study different regional pathways to power, I use Marxist notions of 'modes of production' (economic formations) to model how different bottlenecks channeled resource flows to finance political centrality and inequality (compare Patterson 2009). Here the integrating concepts of production/appropriation, distribution/exchange and consumption provide analytical tools to define the operation of economic formations. My working examples are drawn from my research on historically independent sequences: the Hawaiian archaic states, the highland Andean chiefdoms of the Mantaro Valley, and the Bronze Age chiefdoms of Denmark and western Hungary (Earle 1997; Earle and Kristiansen 2010; Ling et al. 2016). My goal is to show how control over bottlenecks in particular created degrees of political centrality and social inequality, which resulted in specific economic formations. My thesis is that differential control over the economy, based on developing systems of property relationships, created the ability to mobilize staple surpluses and wealth used to craft social institutions with varying structures of inequality and power.

# Channelling Economic Sectors

The political economy requires the channeling of flows in food, labor, wealth, and weapons mobilizing surpluses to support power strategies (Earle and Spriggs 2015). To understand a political economy begins with understanding how agents can channel flows in the general economy. The economy is composed of many interlocking commodity chains of goods and labor that are produced, traded and used. For commodity chains to be important in the political economy, they must 1) involve goods that are of real importance for subsistence, social relationships, and/or ideological meaning in society and 2) have effective bottlenecks (constriction points), by which flows can be channeled to mobilize surpluses.

To understand the general economy requires thinking of its different sectors, each functioning to provide for different human conditions. Analytically I identify four sectors in the general economy: the subsistence economy, the social economy, the political economy and the ritual economy. These sectors are not separate, but they can be split analytically to understand their distinct purposes and dynamics (Earle 2002; Johnson and Earle 2000).

The *subsistence economy* supports human population. It starts with biological needs, providing food, working tools, housing, clothing and the like. The dynamics of the subsistence economy responds to population growth, stability, or even catastrophic collapse. Because population size establishes aggregate subsistence needs, this economic sector is stable, not growth oriented, expanding or contracting as populations change. Variation in the subsistence economy reflects particular opportunities available locally and the technology to exploit them.

The *social economy* organizes human populations. Culturally significant objects serve as gifts to build social relations and things to display social identities. Polanyi envisioned the economy as making and maintaining social structures. The primary basis of the society is the local community and its kinship structure. Objects, typically of local manufacture, mark membership in groups and individual statuses and roles. Additionally individuals give gifts to form regional networks that include trade partners, marriage partners, allies, and patrons. These objects create spheres of interaction. Adam T. Smith (2015) discusses how the engagement in everyday life with stylistically similar objects and their associated behaviors creates a public with emotional commitments to a tribal group. The social economy is fundamentally stable. It provides for the secondary needs of a group to retain the organizational structure needed for its survival (Malinowski 1944).

The subsistence and social sectors of the economy thus provide the means of a society's existence (Polanyi 1957). The apparent stability of these economic sectors is, however, somewhat illusionary, because they offer points of competition, control, and ideological elaboration that become linked to the political economy.

The *political economy* fuels power dynamics in human societies. It mobilizes resources and labor to support frameworks of power, competition, and potential domination. Power relationships on a small scale are found in all societies (Johnson and Earle 2000); however, centralized institutions of governance and control depend systematically on channeled material flows. The political economy creates a dynamic balance of power between social segments. Bottlenecks in the subsistence and social sectors can allow the mobilization of resources and labor to fund the economic, warrior and ideological sources of power (Earle 1997; Earle and Spriggs 2015). Unlike subsistence and social economic sectors, the political economy is fundamentally growth oriented (Johnson and Earle 2000). Positions of political authority yield many personal benefits in lifestyle, access to mates, personal standing in the community, and such. Because of these advantages, competition for these positions is strong, and success in competition depends on an ability to maximize power to fend off opponents. This competition underlies the theory of predatory rule (Levi 1988). The sectors of the general economy should be thought of as possessing bottlenecks, potentially controlled by different groups and thus creating balancing powers among the groups. A Medieval guild of metal workers thus can monopolize skills and knowledge to produce high quality weapons or finery, and, of course, the commoner community controls its own labor required for staple production.

The *ritual economy*, as broadly conceived as ideology, creates meaning and value in human societies (DeMarrais et al. 1996; Wells and Davis-Salazar 2007). Although universal to human societies, re-ligious beliefs have been instituted in highly variable forms ranging from household ritual, to individual shamans, to community rituals of renewal and fertility, and up to large-scale state religious institutions. With the emergence of social complexity, religion provides a key source of power, justifying ruling institutions that they mirror (Durkheim 1915). Expressing awe as power (high devotional attraction; Renfrew 2001), ritual economies are inflationary. As rituals become the new normal, priests and social leaders elaborate them to maintain that awe factor.

The political economy is my focus here, but its articulations with the other sectors are basic to the evolution of social institutions. Particular economic flows channeled by a political economy determined the balance between the different sources of power in society and the relative stability of its political system (Earle 1997). I distinguish between staple-based and wealth-based political economies (D'Altroy and Earle 1985). Blanton and colleagues (1996) envisioned these alternative revenue sources as to their sources – corporate strategies that depended on production from local labor versus network strategies that depended on wealth flows often from outside. Staple-based (corporate) political economies involved local groups with overlapping ownership rights by farmers and their leaders. The primary source of revenues was from the subsistence sector, and mobilized staples supported local rituals considered essential to the fertility and stability of the local group. The means to institute such political economies lay in the built landscape, which materializes the political order. It created a property system allowing mobilization of labor and staples, but requiring chiefs to serve reciprocally their communities in warfare and rituals. Wealth-based (network) political economies depend on the channeling of flows in primitive valuables for the social sector that define status and identity. These involve network strategies, by which leaders seize bottlenecks in production and exchange of wealth objects, set the leaders apart in patterns of consumption; they are thus called exclusionary (Blanton et al. 1996). Typically these wealth items gained special significance by having chiefs incorporate them as props in key rituals. These two strategies of political economies represent alternative means of finance that were intertwined in ways that created particular trajectories of social evolution.

## Staple-based Political Economies

During prehistory, the emergence of complex societies relied first and foremost on the mobilization of staples, especially food, but also items of everyday life such as clothing. The control of bottlenecks in the subsistence sector would, however, have been difficult, because staple commodity chains were short and organized heavily at the household level. Typically such political economies characterized high-density societies, where populations were circumscribed, and land was held as property. By holding property rights, elite segments of society could mobilize surpluses in staples or labor from their commoners. For example, on feudal estates, surfs were provided subsistence allotments in return for labor and/or part of their produce owed to their lord. The origin of these surpluses in local commoner production gave bargaining power to farming communities (Blanton & Fargher 2008).

How difficult this mobilization would have been to maintain is highlighted by Marshall Sahlins' (1972) model of a domestic mode for production (DMP). In traditional societies, households usually had access to its needed resources and provided the labor for most agricultural, herding, and hunting-gathering activities that supported them. The household thus produced the bulk of the goods and services that it consumed. For example, a peasant household in highland Peru produced most of its needs including food, firewood, tools, and housing (Sikkink 2001). The division of labor within the family by age and sex organized work responsibilities. No easy bottlenecks exist in the DMP and so channeling surplus would seem to have been impossible. For most forager societies and many low-density horticultural and pastoral societies, the apparent impossibility of structuring a political economy based on the subsistence sector is evident.

To develop a staple-based political economy required the development of property systems. The most elemental conditions of ownership in traditional societies appear to have been based on labor investment in productive facilities (Johnson and Earle 2000; Earle 2017a). As agriculture was intensified, labor to improve a land's productivity included clearing the forest, maintaining the soil, fencing the fields against animals and the like. This has been called landesque capital (Håkansson and Widgren 2014) – expenditures for land improvement. Such investments by households and larger groups created ownership rights in the improved landscape. These property rights were marked by ancestral cemeteries, which carried inheritance rights to resources across the generations. Such property relations would appear to offer little opportunity for control, and local farmers would always maintain independence except for issues of defense and risk management. Leaders, to whatever degree they existed, would not want to emphasize their distinctiveness by conspicuous consumption.

But strong political economies based on the subsistence sector did emerge along a number of trajectories that can be observed and studied archaeologically. The creation of property rights provided the bottlenecks allowing for the mobilization of a proportion of staple production and community labor. These property regimes materialized in the built landscape could take different forms (economic facilities, defensive works, and ritual monuments) depending on the particular strategic options seized by emergent leaders.

## Hawaiian Island States

Over the last forty years, the prehistory of the Hawaiian Islands has become unusually well documented (Bayman and Dye 2013; Cordy 2000; Kirch (1985, 1990, 2010; Ladefoged and Graves 2008). Through time, Hawaiian chiefs came to form a distinctive class, owning all lands, which they allocated to commoners for their subsistence. A cadre of warriors protected the chiefs and their interests, and priests directed elaborate rituals that portrayed kings and chiefs as living gods. Pristine archaic states formed here a particularly vivid example of social evolution outside the developing world economy (Hommon 2013; Kirch 2010). The relationship between population growth, intensification of production, risk and sustainability, warfare and property relationships created its political economy based on staple finance. The Hawaiian sequence illustrates a high-density society dependent on intensified agriculture with facilities including irrigation. Such societies had autocratic, stable political regimes, what have been referred to as the Asiatic Mode of Production (Marx 1965; Friedman and Rowlands 1977).

In many archaeological sequences, intensification involved engineered landscapes for staple-production. Facilities included terraced fields, irrigation systems, drained fields, fishponds and weirs, and herding corrals and intensive infield hay fields. Such improvements differentiated the landscape into pockets of improved land that were particularly desirable and required defense against outsiders. The building of facilities created the engineered landscape that formed the basis for new property relations so evident in the ethnographic record of traditional societies (Earle 2000). A strong empirical linkage exists, for example, between engineered irrigation landscapes of irrigation and the formation of state societies with distinctive property regimes (Wittfogel 1957). The pristine Hawaiian states document how this linkage can be understood from a political economy perspective (Earle 1978; Earle and Doyle 2008; Earle and Spriggs 2015).

To contextualize this case of pristine state formation requires a brief description of Polynesian prehistory (see Kirch 1990, 2000). Scattered across the Pacific, starting about 1000 BCE, remote island groupings were among the last places on earth to be colonized. Using ingenious sailing canoes, Polynesians explored, discovered and settled almost all inhabitable islands there. From small founding colonist groups, populations expanded, subsistence production intensified, and a rather remarkably, full range of social complexity developed. The result was a natural laboratory of historical experimentation, whereby some societies remained quite simple (almost egalitarian in ethos), while archaic states developed on the Hawaiian Islands and Tonga (Hommon 2013; Kirch 1985, 2010; Sahlins 1958).

The six major Hawaiian Islands are located just below the Tropic of Cancer in the central Pacific and remained physically remote until 'discovered' by Captain Cook in 1778. Polynesian colonists found here rich volcanic and alluvial soils, to which they brought domesticated plants and animals to realize a great agricultural productivity. Developments in Hawaiian society followed trajectories common across the Pacific, but went further to form particularly complex political systems on each major Hawaiian Island. Earle and Spriggs (2015) describe a three-step process:

First, following early colonization about 1000 CE, open lands were generally available to all comers. Populations spread out along the coast, largely dependent on maritime resources and simple horticulture. Settlements were small and scattered along the coast. At this time, no effective land ownership system could have existed. Although individual chiefs might have wanted to claim rights to surplus, supporters could easily have moved away unless inducements were offered to stay close.

Second was the development of local chiefdoms with land ownership held by their individual lineages. Long-term population growth required the spread of settlements both along the coast and into the interior. Clearing the upland forests accelerated erosion, degraded the interior soils, and required an abandonment of interior settlements (Hommon 1986). That same erosion, however, enriched bottomland soils (Spriggs 1997). In geologically older areas of Kauai, Oahu, western Maui and northern Hawai'i, local communities developed irrigated systems, fishponds, tree groves of bananas, breadfruit and coconut, and ritual monuments, pathways, and division walls. Although composed of small-scale systems, these irrigation zones were highly productive pockets, over which ownership could be asserted and defended (Fig. 1). Based on homologous similarities to the Marquesas (Handy 1923) and other Polynesia island groups, each valley or small cluster of valleys probably formed a separate local chiefdom. Lands would have been owned by local corporate lineages and individual families would have held use rights to their plots. Warfare was probably ubiquitous between valley chiefdoms, but the natural valley walls would have provided defenses against neighboring belligerents. In locations without eroded valleys or stream systems, however, irrigation was impossible, and a growing population became dependent on limited, highly productive terraced agricultural zones (Ladefoged et al. 2009). In such environments, no natural defenses for the local community would have existed, and con-quest warfare would have been less constrained. In these cases, chiefs would have been particularly important for defense of lineage land and its developed facilities (compare Kirch 1994, 2010).

Third was the period of inter-community conquest that formed island-wide chiefdoms. Ruling chiefs set out to conquer broad swaths of territory, which had originally been subdivided among separate corporate-lineage chiefdoms. By conquest, the high chiefs cut ancient Polynesian lineage system property rights, and imposed a feudal-like system in which commoners gave obligated labor to chiefs in return for

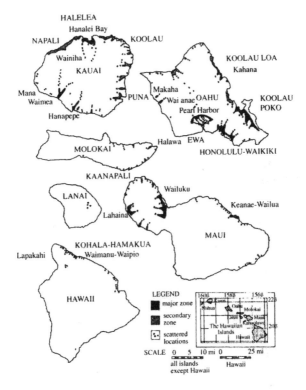

Figure 1. Historic zones of irrigated taro agriculture, Hawaiian Islands (Earle 2002: Fig. 5.1).

access to their former lineage lands (Hommon 2013; Kirch 2010). Based on historical documentation, subsistence plots and house lots were then allocated to commoners, who in returned were obligated to work chiefly lands and fishponds producing surpluses for the ruling class (Earle 1978). The intensified irrigation facilities and similar dryland fields became highly productive and easily controlled zones.

Ownership of irrigated and dryland complexes, obtained and enforced by warrior might, became the bottlenecks in the Hawaiian subsistence economy. Conquest warfare seized these productive facilities. Ownership and investment by the ruling chiefs guaranteed the surplus mobilization in return for subsistence access by commoners. The staples and staple-fed pigs that the commoners produced supported the overarching elite hierarchy and its managerial, warrior, and priestly specialists. The long-term evolution of the Hawaiian state appears to have depended on elevated population density, highly productive agricultural complexes, strong circumscription, and the ability to assert ownership through conquest warfare. Such a system of institutional ownership of intensified landscapes created the circumscription of populations that underlay the emergence of most early states. Carneiro (1970) postulates such a sequence for the irrigation-based states along the desert, coastal fringe of the Andes of South America and in other areas of high population density. The lack of an exit strategy limited the bargaining power of commoners, but chiefly dependency on their labor pressured elites to serve their populations so as to overcome passive resistance.

## Highland Peruvian Hillfort Chiefdoms

In the Andes of highland Peru, following the collapse of the Wari Empire, a distinctive hillfort-building society developed late in prehistory (D'Altroy and Hastorf 2001; Moseley 2001; Arkush and Stanish 2005). Like the Hawaiian case, population growth, agricultural intensification, and warfare were interlocked, but prior to Inca imperial conquest, the society remained fragmented into spatially small-scale chiefdoms, which were in constant conflict with each other. Here a staple-based political economy was grounded on landscape construction that involved fortification to defend communal ownership of improved lands (Earle 1997).

Hillfort societies are known from around the world. Among the Polynesians, the Maori war chiefs were responsible for organizing defense of the community's land. Late in the sequence after sustained population and agricultural expansions, these chiefs organized the construction of major fortifications that asserted lineage land claims and the willingness to defend them against any would-be conqueror or raiders. In these hillforts, the lineage stored its annual sweet potato harvest in special pits. The ownership of land and the central storage again created key opportunities for the chiefs to assert and display their special status. Similar patterns are seen in the many British hillforts built across the landscape during the early Iron Age. Most famous was Maiden Castle, with a complex of four ditch and rampart defensive enclosures that probably dominated a local region. Excavations in these hillforts show frequently many four-post structures that have been interpreted as storage granaries (Cunliffe 1983). The Hungarian tell settlements also fit the hillfort model.

Cross-culturally warfare and community defense are linked variables, which created an opportunity for emerging leaders to coordinate the logistics for large fighting forces for a communal defense (Roscoe 2013). Defensive facilities vary from the relatively egalitarian communal houses of the American Southwestern Pueblos or the Iban long-houses of Borneo, to larger hillfort communities of the European Iron Age or the *pa* of New Zealand Maori, and up to the extensive regional fortification walls and ditches of coastal Peru and other states. Agricultural intensification requires defense of improved lands, and effective defense involved the organization of fighting forces, the recruitment of allies, and the construction of defensive works. Defensive works, I argue, were probably more about property than about fear; they demonstrate the willingness of a group to stand and fight to defend what was theirs.

Archaeologically the key measure of defense of property rights was the labor invested in fortification (Earle 2017a).

I illustrate how a general process of intensification and inter-community warfare created a political economy dominated by war chiefs. Because the tasks of defense, especially at scales represented by the construction of large defensive works, required war leaders, these chiefs probably secured overarching rights to surpluses from community lands needed to fund the cooperative labor that built the facilities. The larger-scale defenses, such as represented by Andean hillforts, were undoubtedly built under direction of chiefs, and these defensive monuments declared both the community's strength, corporate nature, and the war chief's leadership (Roscoe 2013). One common characteristic of hillforts was central storage and defense of the cereal/tuber produce. Thus the fortification can represent two key bottlenecks in the staple economy - corporate ownership of productive land and the centralized flow of staples, for which chiefs could claim some rights over distribution.

State expansion through conquest was forestalled in hillfort-building societies by the highly effective hill-top redoubts that organized local populations against state expansion (Clastres 1977). The key bottleneck in the staple-based political economy was corporate ownership of productive lands, from which the chiefs obtain rights to surplus primarily in matters of war. During peace, the war chiefs were expected to step down, allowing for other largely collective actions to solve problems. While such hillfort societies have sometimes been called egalitarian (Sastre and Sánchez-Palencia 2013), local war chiefs were undoubtedly important and often wanted to expand their power, but the bargaining power of their farmers could keep them in check. I guess that this could be considered a Hillfort Mode of Production.

The Wanka of highland Peru illustrate the growth of hillfort chiefdoms (D'Altroy and Hastorf 2001; Earle 1997; Hastorf 1990, 1993). The Wanka were a cultural group living in the central Mantaro Valley of highland Peru. The Mantaro is a high, intermountain valley (3200 – 4000 m), surrounded by *puna* (grasslands) and glacial mountain peaks. In the valley bottom, maize, quinoa, and now wheat are grown using irrigation. On the surrounding uplands up to about 3800 m, potatoes are produced with rainfall agriculture. Higher still are the puna lands grazed by llama, alpaca and now sheep. The climate is seasonal with warm and wet summers and cold and dry winters. The primary limitations to agricultural production were frost and water that made this zone risky for maize production (Hastorf 1993). By about 1000 CE, the Wanka emerged as a distinct cultural assemblage of independent small-scale polities, which fought among themselves. About 1460 the rapidly expanding Inca Empire conquered the Wanka, which became an imperial province.

During pre-Inca times, Wanka society lived in hilltop settlements made up of stone houses organized into patio groups and surrounded by massive stone fortifications (Fig. 2). These settlements, like Chawín, were impregnable redoubts that could defend local communities and their lands. The development of these hillfort-building chiefdoms followed a rather predictable sequence. During the first Wanka period (1000 – 1250 CE), settlements were fairly small and scattered with modest hillfort settlements (less than 1000 inhabitants). The importance of defense suggests both competition for resources and community property rights over these resources. During the second Wanka period (1250 – 1460 CE), population surged, agricultural production was intensified, and settlements were associated with agricultural facilities that included irrigation, drained fields, ridged fields, and terraces (Hastorf and Earle

Figure 2. Aerial photograph of the Wanka II, hillfort settlement Chawin in the Mantaro Valley, Peru (D'Altroy and Hastorf 2001: Fig. 6.7).

1985). The scale of settlements increased dramatically, and communities were organized into settlement hierarchies with dominant centers of up to 10,000 people and surrounding smaller settlements (Earle 2005). Much like the Hawaiian case, only Inca imperial power broke community property relations by imposing state ownership. Then community lands were allocated back to the Wanka for their subsistence, but only in return for obligated labor owed to the state and used to produce centrally stored staple surpluses, held in the famous Inca warehouses (D'Altroy and Earle 1985).

Detailed historical information on the Wanka chiefs derives from Spanish administrative documents (D'Altroy 1992; Hastorf 1993). The chiefs (*cinche*) were supposed to lead only in war. They organized both inter-community wars of defense and expansion, and when successful they had first rights to conquered parcels and women. Community members were obligated to work the chief's lands, which produced the surplus for the chief's personal support and his war related work. Most visible were the fortification walls that defined the community. Chiefs were not distinguished lavishly, but their house compounds were bigger, probably reflecting polygynous marriages, and they contained evidence of feasting (D'Altroy and Hastorf 2001). Unlike the conquest-oriented warfare of the Hawaiian and Inca examples, community property rights were not abrogated by a ruling sector.

### Early Neolithic Societies of the Atlantic Fringe

As characterized many prehistoric sequences worldwide, a third way to assert property in land has been to construct ceremonial monuments (Artursson et al. 2016). In examples from Anatolia and Japan to Mesoamerica and Peru, ritual monuments were the earliest forms of permanent landscape constructions, often found at quite low population densities. This observation has led some to emphasize that religion (as opposed to economy) was foundational to civilizations, but the role of religion can best be seen as imbedded within the political economy (Earle 1997). I believe that mobilized labor in ritual practice and associated monumental construction created permanent places of religious attraction. Monumental constructions made central places for ceremonies, and these central places would have been strongly identified with the leaders, who organized their construction. Characteristic of low-density societies for which exit strategies would have always existed, a Ritual Model of Production would have operated to attach populations to leaders sponsoring ritual cycles with their permanent, built landscapes.

As described ethnographically, feasting and modest monument constructions have a political dimension allowing for the mobilization of staples and labor (Adams 2004, 2007; Hayden 2014). By building monuments, leaders are able to assert a right to surplus staples and labor from community lands (Earle and Spriggs 2015). In low-density societies where circumscription was absent, ritual monuments appear to have provided an engineered landscape that was in some ways analogous to intensified agricultural facilities and to defensive works as means to tether people to the land and to make them obligated to their leaders. Such monuments are even found in low-density forager societies, where political integration probably helped utilize highly variable resources (O'Shea 2008).

The Atlantic fringe of Europe was characterized in prehistory as a frontier. Agriculture arrived relatively late, population densities were low, and settlement sizes were small. Southern Scandinavia represents well this frontier society, in which surprising complexity emerged. During the Early Neolithic there (4000- 3200 BCE) and elsewhere across the Atlantic Fringe, the sequence of monumental construction illustrates the building of regional ritual formations based on mobilizing labor and staples (Artursson et al. 2016). Following the introduction of farming, population grew modestly to perhaps 1 person/km$^2$ as the forests were partly cleared for farming and animal herding. This forest clearing was a significant capital investment, and local groups materialized their association with improved lands by constructing funerary monuments, establishing in-place inheritance rights of local populations through their ancestors. After 4000 BCE, local groups built and repeatedly used burial monuments that included first long barrows and façade graves followed in the next 600 years by dolmens and megalithic graves, which required substantial crews to lug and erect stone burial chambers. Often new burial chambers would incorporate, or be placed in close proximity with, earlier burial monuments suggesting an association with place and probable long-term corporate rights.

By 3600 BCE, the Scandinavian farmers began to build central gathering places, which continued to be associated with mortuary practices. Assuming that mortuary practices always involved inheritance of status and other rights, such monuments probably materialized a regional system of property, whereby leaders held some claims to surpluses (Artursson et al. 2016). These places had varying assortments of platforms, massive upright timber walls, megalithic alignments, earthen ditches and enclosures, and the like. Most well known are causewayed enclosures. On the Danish Island of Funen, for example, was the enclosure site Sarup I (3400–3200 BCE) (Andersen 1997). It covered 8.5 ha with a palisade, segmented trenches surrounding the palisade, a fenced entrance, and many pits often with ritual deposits (Fig. 3). The palisade was of split oak planks making a solid wall. Other monumental gathering places included the famous cursus and henge monuments in England (Earle 2002). Construction of such monuments would have required hundreds of workers, and I envision the necessity of leaders to mobilize workers and the staples to support them with feasts. The places and associated ceremonies thus became identified with the chiefs who supported their construction and associated ceremonies, and as a result came to hold overarching rights to some surplus.

In sum, the building of the landscape of agricultural facilities, fortification works, and/or ceremonial monuments created an engineered landscape of community property rights. With responsibility for economic, political and religious matters, leaders could sponsor feasts and associated landscape constructions, and by doing this they could lay residual claims to group loyalty, labor, and staple surplus. The different functions of monumental construction (agriculture, defense, and ritual) suggests that the emergent political economy rested on opportunistic assortments of powers over production itself, over protection of productive facilities, and over the ceremonial cycles thought essential for group survival. All were linked to a leader's responsibility for the survival of his community and reciprocally its members' responsibility to support their leader's political agenda.

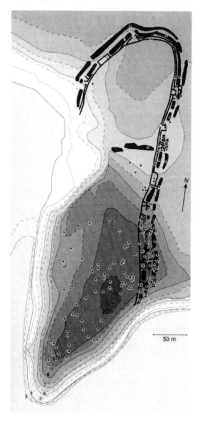

Figure 3. The Early Neolithic causeway enclosure of Sarup I in Denmark. Thin dark line represents the palisade, heavy dark lines are ditches, and dots are pits. The entrance through the palisade and ditches was on the eastern side (Artursson et al. 2016: Fig. 7a).

# Wealth-based Political Economies

During prehistory, complex societies also emerged based on control over prestige goods economies (Friedman and Rowlands 1977). These societies were relatively low-density, requiring political relationships quite different from the higher density, staple-based political economies. The control of bottlenecks in the social sector would have involved various potential bottlenecks in the commodity chains of prestige goods, weapons, and other highly valued objects. Typically such objects were controllable either because they were obtained from a distance or involved technical knowledge. Control over wealth resulted in control over highly valued objects and the means to express meaning in ritual.

The social and ritual sectors of traditional economies involved the production and distribution of special items (primitive valuables) used materially to construct within a ritual context a person's identity and status and to establish networks of kinship, friendship and political alliance. Primitive valuables were always important in public displays associated with feasting and intergroup negotiations. The use of special items is probably universal in human history, but their role changed dramatically with elaborations in political economies. Choices of materials, manufacture methods, and elaborated forms created opportunities to control at least partially the commodity chains for these special items (Earle 2004).

To design a political economy based on the flows of wealth required the presence of bottlenecks in the commodity chains of primitive valuables. In most traditional economies, such control would have been difficult because of alternative objects of significant that were available. Distinctive basketry, pottery, rock art, wooden staffs, images of many materials, clothing and the like could be made of many local or foreign materials and manufacture by many social actors from a spouse to community specialists or ceremonial persons (Spielmann 1998). The decentralized social network that characterized the more egalitarian societies formed a web such that bottlenecks could be easily circumvented.

Control was not, however, impossible, and probably served early on to emphasize social differences. Two elements appear to have worked together to make wealth-based strategies important for emergent political economies. First was the expansion of trade in special objects that could have resulted from self-organizing (bottom-up) desires for the exotic; second was a desire from elites to promote the significance of specific objects that could be more easily controlled. With the increasing volume of trade at a distance, chiefs could emphasize the use of foreign objects, for which constricting access was practical. As discussed for the European Bronze Age, the creation of world systems of trade in metals around the centers of civilization created such opportunities for emergent elites in even low-density situations.

To some measure, all emergent polities, even those relying on a staple-based political economy used primitive valuables to mark significant events and their leaders. The wealth objects of the Hawaiian Island states, for example, defined a ruling class that controlled the political hierarchy, through which staples were mobilized (Earle 1997). The ruling paramount and his chiefs were presented as gods on earth. They wore ceremonial clothes with dramatic colors and decoration that were the dress of the gods. Their feathered capes and helmets featured rainbows arching over the chiefs' shoulders and heads, symbolically demonstrating that a living god was present (Fig. 4). To make these items of personal adornment, tens of thousands of feathers were attached to a wicker base. The dominant color of a paramount's cloak was brilliant yellow, the feathers from the rare O'o, a mountain bird

Figure 4. "Portrait of Kaneena, a Chief of the Sandwich Islands in the North Pacific" by John Webber (1778–1779). The chief is shown wearing his feathered helmet and cloak, representing the arching rainbow over an earthly god.

that displayed small yellow tufts on its flanks. To make the ruler's cloak required the capture of thousands of these elusive birds. Although bird specialists were involved in collection, feathers did not flow through a market-like system, but rather were collected as part of annual tribute. With mobilized staples, chiefs supported attached specialists, who crafted the special paraphernalia that the paramount distributed by size and quality to the hierarchy of supporting chiefs. These cloaks and helmets thus represented visually the system of redistribution in the feudal-like economy of mobilization. Elite clothing was a straightforward material representation of the political economy, in which the divine ruler held ownership of community lands and their people. In such a situation, the wealth items would have been only a minor part of the political economy (Earle 1990).

Like the Hawaiian states, the Andean hillfort chiefdoms of the Wanka relied on a staple-based political economy, but wealth items signify some elements of a social hierarchy (D'Altroy and Hastorf 2001). The households of war chiefs were distinguished by distinctive feasting practices associated with higher frequencies of maize (difficult to grow at high elevation), of serving vessels for maize beer and of burnt bone from roasted meat. The large maize-beer jars were concentrated in elite households; they were stylistically elaborated, often representing a human (sometimes distinctively female) with applique human face at the jar's neck and on the jar body, breast and hands across the belly (Costin 2001). They were both locally produced and traded in from neighboring Wanka groups 15 – 50 km away. Additionally, wealth items included silver and copper disks sewn onto clothing, *tupu* pins used to secure cloaks at the neck, and a scattering of marine shell and special stone beads and pendants worn at the neck (Owen 2001). The copper and malachite were probably obtained from mines in the surrounding region (< 50 km), and the silver, marine shell, and lapis lazuli came from long-distance trade (> 50 km). The low frequency of such material suggests that it was of relatively limited importance in the political economy (for details, see Earle 2001). Social valuables were likely obtained through elite spheres of exchange. Wealth objects among the Wanka evidently marked elite distinction, but they were neither dramatic nor exclusive in their forms and distributions. In simple terms, Wanka war chiefs were not distinguished dramatically in their consumption.

Wealth objects, however, do function to define status distinction based on exoticism and rarity, and this distinction can be foundational to the political economy. Foreign objects are particularly important, because their meaning is easily manipulated because of their unknown or very distant origins. Additionally with the emergence of high-volume trade in wealth, opportunities emerged for control of the bottleneck in the commodity chains that allowed for new prospects to finance political institution with the movement of wealth itself. The archaeological sequence of the Eurasian Bronze Age appears to represent this alternative pathway for political development based on selective control over extensive networks of prestige goods exchange (Sherratt 1993).

### Bronze Age Europe: Wealth-based Political Economies

By 2400 BCE, the expansion of the Bell Beaker phenomenon and metal trade progressively incorporated Europe into a world economy. Although focused on metal, this broad-scale trading economy included amber, spondylus, jet, textiles, salt, slaves, and probably many other wealth objects from many regions. The development of regional specializations and subsequent interchange responded to local comparative advantages based on special products (copper, tin and gold sources), special knowledge (sulfide ore extraction and maritime expertise), and relative position in the expanding networks (Earle et al. 2015). From the Neolithic through the Iron Age, wealth flows became progressively important in the political economy of Eurasia, documenting a profound structural transformation based on changing political economies (Earle and Kristiansen 2010; Frankenstein and Rowlands 1977; Sherratt 1997; Wells 1980). Metal became transformative for weapons, display finery and working tools, and across much of Europe, the new technology required especially the high volume trade in copper and tin, derived from different regions.

A debate has emerged concerning how uniformly important the emergence of metal trade was to Europe in the Bronze Age. While some stress its fundamental transformation (Kristiansen 2012; Kristiansen and Earle 2015), others have emphasized the long-term continuity in societies across the Neolithic-Bronze Age transition (Kienlin 2012). This debate illustrates the potential value of a political economy approach to describe micro-regional variation in social change (Neitzel and Earle 2014). I argue that the specific nature of societies, their subsistence economies, and their articulation with changing trade patterns determined much of the cultural variation observed in the Bronze Age. In locations removed from international trade, staple-based political economies continued largely unchanged, but in areas articulated with high volume flows of metals, prestige goods defined new statuses marked by displays seen in burials and hoards. Six potential bottlenecks existed in wealth-based trade that emergent elites sought to control (Earle et al. 2015):

1. Mining and copper smelting activities offered potential bottlenecks based on ownership of rich mineral resources and/or control over special smelting technologies. In most cases, these potential bottlenecks were apparently not relevant, because the many sources and elemental technology of smelting made them difficult to control. For example, in the Alps during the Early Bronze Age (EBA), no dominant mining centers existed, so copper production here did not result in a local advantage of one group over others (Shennan 1995; Kienlin and Stöllner 2009). Even in the Mitterberg area with its substantial lodes, evidence for elite control is lacking.

2. Available transport routes for the metals and other commodities could constrict flows along dominant routes, and these flows could

thus be partially controlled. Two major BA systems of metal flow seem to have connected northern and southern Europe: the riverine routes of Central Europe and the maritime routes of the Mediterranean and Atlantic fringe. In situations where rivers provided particularly effective, high-volume trade, settled groups acted like the 'robber barons' of the Medieval Age to monitor trading crafts and extract payments for safe passage. Maritime routes would have been more open, but could also have offered potential bottlenecks at good harbors and strategic trans-shipping points.

3. Transport technology could provide elements of control by emerging chiefs and entrepreneurs. The use of water transport, particularly with boats capable of navigating on open oceans, created a need for capital investment, specialized sailors, and warriors' protection. During the Bronze Age, complex sewn-plank boats capable of long-distance sea journeys were developed already on the EBA British Isles (Cunliffe 2001) and in Scandinavia (Ling 2008).

4. Warrior defense of transport routes and traded commodities offered control over the commodity chains of wealth items. In a world without large states able to guarantee safe trade, warriors must have defended the production, movement and storage of wealth and acted as settled raiders and pirates to siphon off wealth along routes (Vandkilde 2006, 2007). Control over warriors, through providing them with weapons and special paraphernalia, thus could result in forceful seizure and defense of bottlenecks.

5. The fabrication of metal artifacts could require highly specialized knowledge and rituals held by only a few craftspeople. The more elaborate the technology, the fewer people would have the required skills, and the easier it would be for elites to control these attached specialists and distribution of their exceptional products (Earle 2002).

6. Potential control of local exports provided another potential bottleneck. Commodities that served as exports during the Bronze Age included agro-pastoral products (horses, cattle hides, wool), special materials (amber, jet, spondylus and soapstone), craft items (such as weapons, jewelry and specialty serving vessels), and probably slaves (Earle and Kristiansen 2010; Ling et al. 2016; Uhnér 2010).

## Contrasting Southern Scandinavia and Western Hungary during the Bronze Age

To develop a political economy that controlled flows of metals and other wealth items required one or more of the bottlenecks described above. In Europe through the Bronze Age and into the Iron Age, much of the micro-regional and temporal variation in social inequality and chiefly power reflected, I argue, variable control opportunities over particular bottlenecks. In southern Scandinavia, for example, we propose a model of political economy called the Scandinavian Mode of Production (SMP) (Ling et al. 2016). To understand the SMP, we start with Marx and Engel's underspecified notion of a Germanic Mode of Production (Marx 1965; Engels 1972; compare Gilman 1995). Envisioned as highly decentralized, families were largely independent economic units owning their farms individually. Free farmers were organized fitfully by chieftains for defense of land and settlement of disputes. SMP involves similarly decentralized social settings, but social stratification and political control emerged based on control over maritime trading and raiding. Here the increasing importance of metal weapons and wealth caused increasing social stratification and chiefly power. In contrast, in western Hungary, a community-based control over transport on the Danube and other major corridors formed compact chiefdoms with heterarchical control over agro-pastoral production and trade. There limited social hierarchy became evident.

*Scandinavian Early Bronze Age.* Migrating into frontier Scandinavian, Neolithic farmers cleared forests for farming and pastoralism. Agriculture was quite marginal and population densities remained low in most of the region until historic times. Despite this frontier location, the region developed remarkable complexity during the Bronze and Iron Ages.

The origin of Scandinavian Bronze Age society lies in the Neolithic. In the Early Neolithic, as discussed previously, ceremonial cycles were linked to the construction of monumental places (Artursson et al. 2016). Already some wealth/symbolic items began appearing in monumental places, ritual depositions and burials. Many of the wealth items were local in origin, including amber beads and polished flint axes, but some long-distance trade included axes of jade, other special stone, and copper (Klassen 2004). During the Middle Neolithic Age, an archaeological assemblage called the Battle Axe Culture probably resulted from both migration and profound shift towards agro-pastoralism as extensive pasturelands were created by the removal of forests. Burial monuments emphasized small individual barrows with male burials containing battle-axes and with female burials containing personal adornments, especially local amber beads. Some long-distance specialty items continued to be imported, but the emphasis on the individual male warrior marked a new ethos for Scandinavian prehistory. I believe that this ethos reflects a warrior complex that characterizes many ethnographically described pastoral societies, in which warriors defended (and seized) moveable wealth in animals (compare Sweet 1965).

By 2000 BCE, the frequency of imported metal wealth objects increased with maritime trade (Vandkilde 2007). The warrior ethos of the society continued, but house locations became permanently established suggesting the creation of independent farms as envisioned for the GMP

(Earle et al. 1998). This Dagger Period had late Bell Beaker connections associated with distinctive flint daggers, arrow points, and ceramic forms. The local use of amber disappeared from burial contexts in southern Scandinavia, presumably exported for international trade (Shennan 1982). Judging from find distributions, Bell Beaker maritime ventures followed the Atlantic fringe into Denmark and then north into Sweden and Norway. It seems reasonable that the extension into the far north may have been linked to the search for wood sources to build boats.

By 1600 BCE, a western maritime route channeled metals from the copper mines of Spain and Sardinia in the south and copper and tin from British Isles and Ireland to meet the expanding demand for metal in southern Scandinavian (Earle et al. 2015). In Thy, located in northern Jutland, a remarkable concentration of metal wealth appeared in the EBA (Kristiansen 1978). Showing marked social inequality, burials contained metal swords, daggers and other paraphernalia materializing a warrior class with chiefly lords. Especially elaborated were the highly decorated chiefly swords. Chiefly halls (over 30 m long), like those found in Sønderhå parish in Thy, dominated a dispersed low-density settlement of farmhouses (18 m). A similar distinction emerged in the distribution of barrows that covered the highlands of the region; many were quite low (less than 1 m), but a few, like Baunehøj, stood prominently over 4 m tall (Fig. 5).

To understand the emergent of significant social stratification in southern Scandinavia, the SMP can be seen as containing the following elements (Ling et al. 2016):

- Low-density populations interconnected by exchanges of wealth;
- Warriors able to raid, trade, and protect wealth;
- Agricultural sector with productive lands, and autonomous households owned by free farmers;

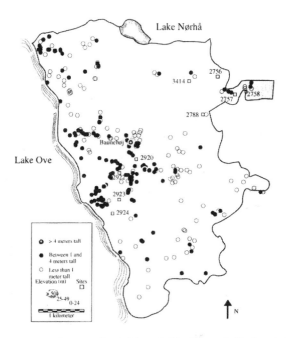

Figure 5. Barrow distribution in Sønderhå parish, Thy, Denmark. The farm indicated by site 3414 was the location of two sequential chiefly halls. The large barrow of Baunhøj dominates the landscape (Earle 2002: Fig. III.2)

- Slaves to expand surplus production on chiefly farms;
- Maritime sector with timber and specialized knowledge to construct and crew boats;
- Ownership of boats by chiefs, who had supported their construction;
- Chiefly finance of entrepreneurial voyages;
- Manning of boats by mariners and warriors, overseen by a chiefly captain;

- Raiding along voyaging routes for slaves and other valuables to be traded for wealth;
- Transfer of metals and slaves to chieftains, who owned boats and financed voyages; and
- Gift exchanges by chieftains to establish networks of power and alliance.

For Scandinavia a positive growth cycle was apparently established with agricultural intensification, expanding raiding-trading voyaging, wealth accumulation and distribution, and the creation of networks of power spread over regions. Foundational was the economic power exercised through ownership of large farms and sponsorship of voyaging. Warrior power was instrumental to protect and extend chiefly lands and wealth movement and to seize slaves. Economic surpluses, which were invested in weapons and boats, allowed chiefs to fix warriors to chiefly interests, as these warriors also pursued their personal social advancement. And then ideological power gave meaning and legitimacy to chieftains and warrior service. With economic surpluses, chiefs supported feasts and ritual specialists in ceremonies to mitigate risks of distant voyaging and warfare. Objects took on special value by the ritual contexts in which they served. The rock art illustrates the ritual significance of the political economy. Chiefs also supported woodworkers to ornament houses and boats with elaborate carving imbued with status and religious significance. In the SMP, the three sources of power were intertwined to fashion chieftaincies and confederacies.

A key element in the model is the importance of slaves. The SMP has been based on the historical specificity of the Viking case and applied to BA Scandinavia as a means to resolve key inconsistencies in our understanding of the ancestral Scandinavian Bronze Age. We know that slaves were essential to the Vikings (Brink 2008; Ling et al.

2016). Obtained in systematic raiding through Europe, they provided needed labor on farms, especially the larger chiefly farms, and as an exchange commodity for wealth, especially metals. Slaves in Bronze Age Scandinavia appears to have been important to give Scandinavia the comparative advantage in international trade that would bring in substantial amounts of metal for weapons, finery, and working tools. Although amber has long been thought to have been the major export, the volume of amber would have been inadequate to balance the high volumes of consumed metals as estimated from the archaeological record (Ling et al. 2016). Slaves obtained in entrepreneurial raiding would fill the gap as it did during the Viking period. This hypothesis is suggested to encourage research on slaves in the archaeological data, and the new potential for DNA and strontium studies of human skeletal material would seem a future research direction.

What bottlenecks allowed for the creating of a stratified society in southern Scandinavia? In Thy, the large chiefly burials and halls were distributed according to the best pastureland. Large chiefly farms appeared to have geared up agro-pastoral production to provide an investable surplus. Here the primary bottleneck would have been the ownership of the intensified landscape. I have argued that the barrows in particular defined a new property system, in which warrior-farmers controlled land used for raising cattle and oxen as working animals, meat and hide that were exported (Earle 2002).

But where did the chiefly farms of Thy export their surplus agro-pastoral products, and how did they obtain the extraordinary wealth found here in the EBA? Although the animals might have been driven south towards Germany, as they were in Medieval times, the comparative advantage in animal production between Jutland and Germany at this time is at best unclear. Rather surplus grains and animal products from

Thy may have been exported to the north where the agro-pastoral farms of western Sweden and Norway were more marginal. In our model, we argue that the northern areas of Scandinavia had a strong comparative advantage in wood and a maritime history of seafaring. Thus the exported surpluses from Thy could have supported the production of sea-worthy boats in northern, forested regions (Ling et al. 2016). By financing boat construction, Thy chiefs could have been their owners, the financers of their trading-raiding ventures, and thus the primary recipient of the metal wealth obtained from the south.

The elaborate rock art tradition of BA Scandinavia is found in agriculturally marginal, northern zones, where it depicts thousands of sea-worthy boats (Fig. 6). The proportions of the hull, stem, and prows on the rock-art ships correspond closely with the sewn and plank-built boat from Hjortspring (dated to 350 BCE), which when reproduced and paddled experimentally has proven sea-worthy and capable of long-distance travels (Crumlin-Pedersen 2003). On the coastal rock panels, boat motifs with elaborate prows typically have 6-14 paddling warriors/mariners (Ling 2008). The rock art shows chiefs and warriors armed with bronze swords, axes and spears as typified the burials on Thy. The Scandinavian Mode of Production relied, I argue, on a triad of bottlenecks involving ownership of intensified agro-pastoral lands, sea-worthy boats, and the warriors to protect them.

*Hungarian Early and Middle Bronze Ages along the Danube.* Hungary in prehistory was a rich agrarian region in central Europe. Occupied by farmers and herders early in the Neolithic, a long history exists of settled life with some sizeable villages. Productive agriculture allowed for locally high population densities, and the region was engaged early with regional and international trade (Earle and Kolb 2010; Sherratt

Figure 6. Bronze Age rock art panel from Tanum, Sweden showing boats with decorative prows and sterns and with paddlers indicated by upright lines. Warriors stand with bronze weapons (Kristiansen, personal collection).

1997). Despite its central location and in contrast to Scandinavia, Hungarian society retained a fairly egalitarian ethos well into the Bronze Age (Kienlin 2015).

Hungary during the Bronze Age witnessed a variable but distinctive political economy. Following early colonization by Neolithic people, shifting cultivation with short-term settlements became the norm on fertile loess soils, and a regional specialization developed between primary farming and pastoral zones (Sherratt 1997). In eastern Hungary on fertile alluvial soils of the Tisza River and its tributaries, long-term tell settlements formed in the Late Neolithic. Here communities were probably depending on warrior chiefs to defend corporate ownership of productive lands, as signaled by cemeteries and fortifications. After a period of abandonment in the Copper Age, these eastern tells were occupied again, and a pattern of relatively egalitarian communities continued (Kienlin 2015). In contrast, along the Danube of western Hungary, no tells existed during the Neolithic, but, starting in the EBA, a string of fortified settlements were founded along the bluffs of the River Danube (Uhnér 2010).

The articulation with trade appears to have been of great significance in the Hungarian Bronze Age along the major trade routes. Childe (1929) stressed the importance of rivers, especially the Danube, as transportation routes for metals. Here Bell Beaker traders are to be found. Later along the Danube's bluffs in Hungary and along other major waterways, fortified tells and hillforts arose in the EBA and MBA. In many ways these settlements are reminiscent of the Neolithic tells of eastern Hungary, but their placement on the river bluffs is different. Rather than defining and defending agricultural land, which would have resulted in their placement central to the rich loess soils, their placement above the rivers allowed communities to assert the same corporate ownership over the river itself. These fortifications on the Danube manufactured a new bottleneck—ownership of a segment of the heavily used river route for metal and other commodities that allowed for the extraction of some tribute from traders (Earle and Kolb 2010).

Along the Danube, the larger fortified tell settlements appear to have dominated settlement hierarchies, probably indicating chiefdom-like regional polities (Earle and Kolb 2010). Wealth in metal was accumulated, but, unlike the Scandinavian case, it was not distributed individually among warrior chiefs and lords. Rather wealth occurred as communal hoards in the settlements along the river routes of Hungary and Slovakia and at mouths of Alpine rivers (Earle et al. 2015). Why then were no chiefly burials here? I suggest that the power of chiefs in central Europe was structurally restrained, much like the Wanka war chiefs of the Andes. Thus the distinction gained from the accumulation of wealth was not used to distinguish individuals, but was used ritually to distinguish the power of local political groupings.

The conclusion of a comparison across Europe during the Bronze Age suggests: 1) the metal trade transformed the nature of society (Kristiansen and Earle 2015), but 2) the local nature of this transformation was channeled by both the specific articulations with the trade and social history. The second point is essential to understand Kienlin's (2015) argument that when positioned away from primary transport routes, metal trade did not change everyday life significantly. Even where fortified tell above the Danube extracted wealth, it served to define community, not individual status. Control over commodity chains of special goods helped develop specific spheres of exchange dominated by leaders, but the use of the valuables were dependent on the structure of the social systems. Human societies are the product of human action. The material base is essential for how the political economy affects power structures and inequality, but the relations of production are not predetermined.

## The Possible Relevance of Archaeology
## to Public Discourse and Social Policy

In the modern world, a new consensus has emerged that economic inequality and autocracy are dramatically linked and relentlessly increasing (Piketty 2014). They affect tragically our living standards, democratic principles, and class stratification (Wilkinson and Pickett 2010). Archaeologists may be able to provide a unique long-term perspective on the critical social linkage between economic, social, and power inequalities (Flannery and Marcos 2012). We should probably not search for the origins of autocracy and inequality, which were grounded in our deepest ancestry; rather we can focus on the social processes responsible for their expansion and institutionalization across the *longue durée*. Key is to evaluate the relative increase, stability or decline in social stratification through time. Here archaeologists can provide an important perspective to international discussions of autocracy and inequality that can help formulate novel solutions to the problems associated with troubling modern trends.

What lessons for the modern age are to be learned from archaeological analysis? Strong central power and conspicuous inequalities in wealth and health outcomes are neither natural nor essential to human societies. They are human artifacts that reflect particular forms of political economy. What is equally important is that under similar economic conditions, the legal structure of society can result in very different outcomes. The assumption of modern economic theory that human demands are unlimited is simply wrong (Earle 2017b). Demand is an outcome of conspicuous consumption, which is a particular characteristic of modern capitalism (Veblen 1931). We should not view the world's existing capitalist economy as predetermined or natural, but rather as part of our creation that can be ingeniously altered. Humans build their own histories, or as V. Gordon Childe (1951) expressed in homage to Marx: "Man makes himself."

As archaeologists, how can we help construct a better destiny for humanity? The archaeologist's comparative perspective shows the extremely wide range of social forms that humans have created. These cases from history and prehistory, like the Hawaiian states, the Wanka hillfort chiefdoms and the European trading societies are each social experiments with vastly different characteristics of social inequality, sustainability, and structural fragility. We can break assumptions of economic predestination and the political power of entrenched class-based privilege (Blanton and Fargher 2008). Archaeologists know that there is no end to history, only processes that make and break societies. There is a need, I feel, for prehistorians and historians to engage as public intellectuals to help imagine innovative alternatives for a new world order that lessens inequality both nationally and internationally.

# References

**Adams, R. 2004.**
An Ethnoarchaeological Study of Feasting in Sulawesi, Indonesia. *Journal of Anthropological Archaeology* 23: 56–78.

**Adams, R., 2007.**
Maintaining Cohesion in House Societies of West Sumba, Indonesia. In: Beck, R. ed. *The Durable House: House Society Models in Archaeology.* Southern Illinois University Press, Carbondale, IL, pp. 344–362.

**Andersen, N.H. 1997.**
*The Sarup Enclosures, Sarup Vol. 1.* Højbjerg, Denmark: Jutland Archaeological Society Publications XXXIII.

**Arkush, E., & Stanish, C. 2005.**
Interpreting Conflict in the Ancient Andes: Interpretations for the Archaeology of Warfare. *Current Anthropology* 46: 3-28.

**Artursson, M., Earle, T., & Brown, J. 2016.**
Construction of Monumental Landscapes in Low-density Societies: New Evidence from the Early Neolithic of Southern Scandinavia. *Journal of Anthropological Archaeology* 41: 1-18.

**Bayman, J., & Dye, T. 2013.**
*Hawaii's Past in a World of Pacific Islands.* Washington, DC: SAA Press.

**Blanton, R., & Fargher, L. 2008.**
*Collective Action in the Formation of Pre-Modern States.* New York: Springer.

**Blanton, R., Feinman, G., Kowalewski, S., & Peregrine, P. 1996**
A Dual-Processual Theory for the Evolution of Mesoamerican Civilization. *Current Anthropology* 37: 1– 14.

**Brink, S. 2008.**
Slavery in the Viking Age. In *The Viking World.* Brink, Stefan & Price, Neil eds. Abingdon: Routledge, pp. 49-57.

**Carballo, D., Roscoe, P., & Feinman, G. 2014.**
Cooperation and Collective Action in the Cultural Evolution of Complex Societies. *Journal of Archaeological Method and Theory* 21: 98-133.

**Carneiro, R. 1970.**
A Theory of the Origin of the State. *Science* 169: 733-38.

**Childe, V. G. 1929.**
*The Danube in Prehistory.* Oxford: Clarendon Press.

**Childe, V. G. 1942.**
*What Happened in History?* Baltimore: Penguin.

**Childe, V. G. 1951.**
*Man Makes Himself.* London Watts.

**Clastres, P. 1977.**
*Society Against the State.* New York: Urizen.

**Cobb, C. 1993.**
Archaeological Approaches to the Political Economy of Non-stratified Societies. *Archaeological Method and Theory* 5: 43-100.

**Cordy, R. 2000.**
*Exalted Sits the Chief:* The Ancient History of the Hawaiian Islands. Honolulu: Mutual.

**Costin, C. 2001.**
Production and Exchange of Ceramics. In D'Altroy, T. & Hastorf, C. *Empire and Domestic Economy.* New York: Kluwer Academic, pp. 203-242.

**Cunliffe, B. 1983.**
*Danebury: Anatomy of an Iron Age Hillfort.* London: Bratsford.

**Cunliffe, B. 2001.**
*Facing the Ocean: The Atlantic and Its Peoples, 8000 BC–AD 1500.* Oxford: Oxford University Press.

**Crumlin-Pedersen, O. 2003.**

The Hjortspring Boat in a Ship-Archaeological Context. In O. Crumlin-Pedersen and A. Trakadas, A. eds. *Hjortspring. A Pre-Roman Iron-Age Warship in Context.* Roskilde, Denmark: Ships and Boats of the North 5, pp. 209-32.

**Dalton, G. 1969.**

Theoretical Issues in Economic Anthropology. *Current Anthropology* 10: 63-102.

**Dalton, G. 1977.**

Aboriginal Economies in Stateless Societies. In T. Earle, T., and Ericson, J. eds. *Exchange Systems in Prehistory.* New York: Academic Press, pp. 191-212.

**D'Altroy, T. 1992.**

*Provincial Power in the Inka Empire.* Washington, D.C.: Smithsonian Institute.

**D'Altroy, T., & Earle, T. 1985.**

Staple Finance, Wealth Finance, and Storage in the Inka Political Economy. *Current Anthropology* 26: 187–206.

**D'Altroy, T. & Hastorf, C. 2001.**

*Empire and Domestic Economy.* New York: Kluwer Academic.

**Durkheim, Emile. 1915.**

*The Elemental Forms of Religious Life.* London: Allen & Unwin.

**Earle, T. 1978.**

*Economic and Social Organization of a Complex Chiefdom.* University of Michigan, Anthropological Papers, vol. 63. Ann Arbor: University of Michigan.

**Earle, T. 1990.**

Style and Iconography as Legitimation in Complex Chiefdoms. In M. Conkey and C. Hastorf eds. *The Uses of Style in Archaeology.* Cambridge: Cambridge, pp. 73-81.

**Earle, T. 1997.**

*How Chiefs Come to Power.* Stanford: Stanford University Press.

**Earle, T. 2000.**

Archaeology, Property, and Prehistory. *Annual Review of Anthropology* 29: 39-60.

**Earle, T. 2001.**

Exchange and Social Stratification in the Andes: the Xauxa Case. In T. D'Altroy and C. Hastorf eds. *Empire and Domestic Economy.* New York: Kluwer Academic/ Plenum Publishers, pp. 297-314.

**Earle, T. 2002.**

*Bronze Age Economics.* Boulder: Westview Press.

**Earle, T. 2005.**

The Tunanmarca Polity of Highland Peru and its Settlement System (AD 1350-1450). In R. Blanton (ed.), *Settlement, Subsistence, and Social Complexity.* Los Angeles: Cotsen Institute for Archaeology, University of California, pp. 89-118.

**Earle, T. 2017a.**

Property in Prehistory. In Lionel Smith ed. *Comparative Property Law: Global Perspectives.* Northampton, MA: Elgar, pp. 3-25.

**Earle, T. 2017b.**

Wealth Inequality and the Pristine Hawaiian State: a Political Economy Approach. *Origini* XXXVIII (2015-2): 201-216.

**Earle, T., Beck, J.H., Kristiansen, K., Aperlo, P., Kelertas, K., & Steinberg, J. 1998.**

The Political Economy of Late Neolithic and Early Bronze Age Society: the Thy Archaeological Project. *Norwegian Archaeological Review* 31: 1-28.

**Earle, T. & Doyle, D. 2008.**

The Engineered Landscapes of Irrigation. In L. Cliggett and C. Pool eds. *Economics and the Transformation of Landscape.* Lanham, MD: AltaMira Press, pp.19-46.

**Earle, T., Ling, J., Uhnér, C., Stos-Gale, Z., & L. Lelheim. 2015.**

The Political Economy and Metal Trade in Bronze Age Europe: Understanding Regional Variability in Terms of Comparative Advantages and Articulations. *European Journal of Archaeology 18* (1): 1-25.

**Earle, T., & Kolb, M. 2010.**

Regional Settlement Patterns. In T. Earle and K. Kristiansen eds. *Organizing Bronze Age Societies.* Cambridge: Cambridge University Press, pp. 57-86.

Earle, T., & Kristiansen, K. 2010.
*Organizing Bronze Age Societies.* Cambridge: Cambridge University Press.

Earle, T., & Spriggs, M. 2015.
A Marxist Approach to Pacific Sequences. *Current Anthropology* 56 (4): 515-544.

Engels, F. 1883.
Karl Marx's funeral. *Der Sozialdemokrat,* March 22.

Engels, F. 1972.
*The Origin of the Family, Private Property and the State.* New York: Pathfinder.

Flannery, K., & Marcus, J. 2012.
*The Creation of Inequality.* Cambridge, MA: Harvard University Press.

Frankenstein, S. & Rowlands, M. 1978.
The Internal Structure and Regional Context of Early Iron Age Society in Southwestern Germany. *Bulletin of the Institute of Archaeology* 15: 73-112.

Friedman, J., & Rowlands, M. 1977.
Notes Towards an Epigenetic Model of the Evolution of "Civilization." In J. Friedman & M. Rowlands, eds. *The Evolution of Social Systems.* London: Duckworth, pp. 201-276.

Gilman, A. 1995.
Prehistoric European Chiefdoms: Rethinking "Germanic" Societies. In T. Douglas Price and Gary Feinman, eds. *Foundations of Social Inequality.* Plenum, New York: Gluckman, pp. 235-251.

Håkansson, N.T., & Widgren, M., eds. 2014.
*Landesque Capital: The Historical Ecology of Enduring Landscape Modifications.* Walnut Creek, CA: Left Coast Press.

Handy, E.S.C. 1923.
*The Native Culture in the Marquesas.* Honolulu: Bernice P. Bishop Museum Bulletin 9.

Hastorf, C. 1990.
One Path to the Heights: Negotiating Political Inequality in the Sausa of Peru. In S. Upham (ed.), *The Evolution of Political Systems.* Cambridge: Cambridge University Press, pp. 146-176.

Hastorf, C. 1993.
*Agriculture and the Onset of Political Inequality before the Inka.* Cambridge: Cambridge University Press.

Hastorf, C., & Earle, T. 1985.
Intensive Agriculture and the Geography of Political Change in the Upper Mantaro Region, Peru. In I. S. Farrington ed. *Prehistoric Intensive Agriculture in the Tropics.* BAR International Series 232, pp. 569-595.

Hayden, B. 2014.
*The Power of Feasts.* Cambridge: Cambridge University Press.

Hommon, R. 1986.
Social Evolution in Ancient Hawaii. In P. Kirch (ed.), *Island Societies.* Cambridge: Cambridge University Press, pp. 55-68.

Hommon, R. 2013.
*The Ancient Hawaiian State: Origins of a Political Society.* New York: Oxford University Press.

Johnson, A. & Earle, T. 2000.
*The Evolution of Human Societies.* Stanford: Stanford University Press. (2nd edition)

Kienlin, T. 2012.
Beyond Elites: An Introduction. In Kienlin, T., & Zimmerman, A., eds. *Beyond Elites: Alternatives to Hierarchical Systems in Modeling Social Formations.* Bonn: Habelt, pp. 15-32.

Kienlin, T. 2015.
*Bronze Age Tell Communities in Context.* Oxford: Archaeopress.

Kienlin, T., & Stöllner, T. 2009.
Singen Copper, Alpine Settlement and Early Bronze Age Mining: Is There a Need for Elites and Strongholds? In: T.L. Kienlin and B.W. Roberts, eds. *Metals and Societies. Studies in Honour of Barbara S. Ottaway.* Bonn: Rudolf Habelt, pp. 67- 104.

Kirch, P. 1984.
*The Evolution of the Polynesian Chiefdoms.* Cambridge: Cambridge University Press.

54

Kirch, P. 1985.
Feathered Gods and Fishhooks: An Introduction to Hawaiian Archaeology. Berkeley: California University Press.

Kirch, P. 1990.
The Evolution of Sociopolitical Complexity in Prehistoric Hawaii: An Assessment of the Archaeological Evidence. Journal of World Prehistory 4: 311-345,

Kirch, P. 1994.
The Wet and the Dry: Irrigation and Agricultural Intensification in Polynesia. Chicago: Chicago University Press.

Kirch, P. 2000.
On the Road of the Winds: An Archaeological History of the Pacific Islands before European Contact. Berkeley: University of California Press.

Kirch, P. 2010.
How Chiefs Became Kings: Divine Kingship and the Rise of Archaic States in Ancient Hawai'i. Berkeley: University of California Press.

Klassen, L., 2004.
Jade und Kupfer. Untersuchungen zum Neolitisierungsprozess im westlichen Ostseeraum unter besonderer Berücksichtigung der Kulturentwicklung Europas 5500-3500 BC. Moesgård: Jutland Archaeological Society.

Kristiansen, K. 1978.
The Consumption of Wealth in Bronze Age Denmark: A Study in the Dynamics of Economic Processes in Tribal Societies. In K. Kristiansen and C. Paludan-Müller (eds.), New Directions in Scandinavian Archaeology. Copenhagen: National Museum of Denmark, pp. 158-190.

Kristiansen, K. 2012.
Bronze Age Dialectics: Ritual Economies and the Consolidation of Social Divisions. In Kienlin, T. & Zimmerman, A., eds. Beyond Elites: Alternatives to Hierarchical Systems in Modeling Social Formations. Bonn: Habelt, pp. 381-92.

Kristiansen, K., & Earle, T. 2015.
Neolithic versus Bronze Age Social Formations: A Political Economy Approach. In Kristiansen, K., Smejda, L., & Turek, J., eds. Paradign Found: Archaeological Theory Present, Past and Future. Oxford: Oxbow Books, pp. 234-47.

Ladefoged, T., & Graves, M. 2008.
Variable Development of Dryland Agriculture in Hawai'i. Current Anthropology 49: 359-373.

Ladefoged, T., Kirch, P., Gon, S., Chadwick, O., Hartshorn, A., & Vitousek, P. 2009.
Opportunities and Constraints for Intensive Agriculture in the Hawaiian Archipelago Prior to European Contact. Journal of Archaeological Sciences 36: 2374-83.

Levi, M. 1988.
O Rules and Revenue. Berkeley: University of California Press.

Ling, J. 2008.
Elevated Rock Art — Towards a Maritime Understanding of Bronze Age Rock Art in Northern Bohuslän, Sweden. Gothenburg: GOTARC.

Ling, J., Earle, T., & Kristiansen, K. 2016.
Bronze Age Maritime Chiefdoms and Long-Distance Trade. Paper presented in the conference Trade Before Civilization, 27-28 May, Gothenburg, Sweden.

Malinowski, B. 1944.
The Scientific Theory of Culture and Other Essays. Chapel Hill: University of North Carolina Press.

Marx, K. 1965.
Pre-Capitalist Economic Formations, E. Hobsbawm (ed.). New York: International Publishers.

Marx, K. 1967 [1867].
The Process of Capitalist Production, Vol. 1 of Capital: A Critique of Political Economy. New York: International.

McGuire, Randall H. 2008.
Marxism. In R. Bentley, H. Maschner, & C. Chippindale, eds. Handbook of Archaeological Theory. Lanham, MD: Altamira, pp. 73-93.

Moseley, M. 2001.
> The Incas and their Ancestors: The Archaeology of Peru. London: Thames & Hudson.

Neitzel, J., & Earle, T. 2014.
> Dual-tier Approach to Societal Evolution and Types. Journal of Anthropological Archaeology 36:181-95.

O'Shea, J., 1989.
> The role of wild resources in small-scale agricultural systems. In: Halstead, P., O'Shea, J. (Eds.), Bad Year Economics: Cultural Responses to Risk and Uncertainty. Cambridge: Cambridge University Press, pp. 57–67.

Owen, B. 2001.
> The Economy of Metal and Shell Wealth Goods. In T. D'Altroy and C. Hastorf eds. Empire and Domestic Economy. New York: Kluwer Academic/Plenum Publishers, pp. 265-293.

Patterson, T. 2009.
> Karl Marx, Anthropologist. Oxford: Berg.

Piketty, T. 2014.
> Capital in the Twenty-First Century. Cambridge, MA: Harvard University Press.

Polanyi, K.1957.
> The Economy as Instituted Process. In Polanyi, K., Arensberg, C., & Pearson, H., eds. Trade and Market in the Early Empires. New York: Free Press, pp. 243-270.

Radcliffe-Brown, A.R. 1952.
> Structure and Function in Primitive Society. Glencoe, IL: Free Press.

Renfrew, C., 2001.
> Production and Consumption in a Sacred Economy: The Material Correlates of High Devotional Expression at Chaco Canyon. American Antiquity 66 (1): 14–25.

Ricardo, D. 1817.
> The Principles of Political Economy and Taxation. New York: Dutton.

Roscoe, P. 2013.
> War, Collective Action, and the 'Evolution' if Human Polities. In D. Carballo (ed.), Cooperation and Collective Action. Boulder: University of Colorado Press, pp. 57-82.

Sahlins, M. 1958.
> Social Stratification in Polynesia. Seattle: University of Washington Press.

Sahlins, M. 1972.
> Stone Age Economics. Chicago: Aldine.

Saitta, D. 2005.
> Marxism, tribal society and the dual nature of archaeology. Rethinking Marxism 17:385-397.

Sastre, I., & Sánchez-Palencia, F.J. 2013.
> Nonhierarchical Approaches to the Iron Age Societies: Metals and Inequality in the Castro Culture of the Northwestern Iberian Peninsula. In Cruz, M., García, L., & Gilman, A. The Prehistory of Iberia: Debating Early Social Stratification and the State. London: Routledge, pp. 292-310.

Shennan, S. 1982.
> Exchange and Ranking: The Role of Amber in the Earlier Bronze Age. In Renfrew, C., & Shennan, S., eds. Ranking, Resources, and Exchange. Cambridge: Cambridge University Press, pp. 33-45.

Shennan, S. 1995.
> Bronze Age Copper Producers of the Eastern Alps: Excavations at St. Veit-Klinglberg. Bonn: Habelt.

Sherratt, A.G. 1993.
> What Would a Bronze-Age World System Look Like? Relations between Temperate Europe and the Mediterranean in Later Prehistory. Journal of European Archaeology 1(2): 1–57.

Sherratt, A.G. 1997.
> Economy and Society in Prehistoric Europe. Edinburgh: Edinburgh University Press.

Sikkink, L. 2001.
> Ethnoarchaeology and Contemporary Domestic Economy in the Mantaro Valley. In D'Altroy, T. & Hastorf, C., eds. Empire and Domestic Economy. New York: Kluwer, pp. 97-111.

Smith, A. 1937 (1776).
> An Inquiry into the Nature and Causes of the Wealth of Nations. New York: Modern Library.

Smith, A.T. 2015.
> The Political Machine: Assembling Sovereignty in the Bronze Age Caucasus. Princeton: Princeton University Press.

Spielmann, K. 1998.
> Ritual Craft Specialists in Middle Range Societies. In C. Costin and R. Wright (eds.), Craft and Identity. Washington, DC: Archaeological Papers of the American Anthropological Association 1, pp. 153-159.

Spriggs, M. 1984.
> Marxist Perspectives in Archaeology. Cambridge: Cambridge University Press.

Spriggs, M. 1997.
> Landscape Catastrophe and Landscape Enhancement: Are either or both True in the Pacific? In P. Kirch & T. Hunt, eds. Historical Ecology in the Pacific Islands: Prehistoric Environmental and Landscape Change. New Haven, CT: Yale University Press, pp. 80–104.

Sweet, L. Camel
> Pastoralism in North Arabia and the Minimal Camping Unit. In Leeds, A., & Vayda, A. Man, Culture and Animals. Washington: AAAS Publication 78, pp. 129-52.

Trigger, B. 1980.
> Gordon Childe: Revolutions in Archaeology. London: Thames and Hudson.

Uhnér, C. 2010.
> Makt och Samhälle. Politisk Ekonomi under Bronsåldern i Karpaterbäckenet. Gothenburg: GOTARC.

Vandkilde, H. 2006.
> Archaeology and War: Presentations of Warriors and Peasants in Archaeological Interpretations. In: T. Otto, H. Thrane & H. Vandkilde, eds. Warfare and Society: Archaeological and Social Anthropological Perspectives. Aarhus: Aarhus University Press, pp. 57–75.

Vandkilde, H. 2007.
> Culture and Change in Central European Prehistory, 6th to 1st Millennium BC. Aarhus: Aarhus University Press.

Veblen, T. 1931.
> The Theory of the Leisure Class: An Economic Study of Institutions. New York: Modern Library.

Wells, C., & Davis-Salazar, K. 2007.
> Mesoamerican Ritual Economy. Boulder: University Press, Colorado.

Wells, P. 1980
> Culture Contact: Early Iron Age Europe and the Mediterranean World. Cambridge: Cambridge University Press.

Wilkinson, R., & Pickett, K. 2010.
> The Spirit level: Why Equality is Better for Everyone. London: Penguin books.

Wittfogel, K. 1957.
> Oriental Despotism. New Haven: Yale University Press.